The Neglected Qualification

The Neglected Qualification

Black Sheep in Pastors' Homes

Douglas Wilson

canonpress
Moscow, Idaho

Douglas Wilson, *The Neglected Qualification: Black Sheep in Pastors' Homes*
Copyright ©2015 by Douglas Wilson

Published by Canon Press
P. O. Box 8729, Moscow, Idaho 83843
800-488-2034 | www.canonpress.com

Cover design by James Engerbretson.
Interior design by Valerie Anne Bost.

Unless otherwise indicated, all Scripture quotations are from the King James Version.

Table of
Contents

The Shallow End of the Pool

For various reasons, we need to spend some time considering what might be called "the neglected qualification." The spiritual state of the preacher's kids has long been proverbial, and not in a good way, and yet we continue to have the following in our Bibles.

"A bishop then must be blameless, the husband of one wife . . . One that ruleth well his own house, having his children in subjection with all gravity; (For if a man know not how to rule his own house, how shall he take care of the church of God?) (1 Tim. 3:2,4-5).

"For this cause left I thee in Crete, that thou shouldest set in order the things that are wanting, and ordain elders in every city, as I had appointed thee: If any be blameless, the husband of one wife, having faithful children not accused of riot or unruly. For a bishop must be blameless . . ." (Tit. 1:5-7).

The majority of the Christian world has work-arounds and explanations for these verses, while the minority that wants them to mean what they appear to mean, sometimes applies them in a wooden or legalistic fashion. While wanting to avoid both extremes, we still need to affirm that these words mean *something*, and that they apply *sometime*. I want to explore what that something might mean, and when that sometime might be.

Let us throw all the difficult cases on the table right away. This is talking about making someone an elder, not talking about someone who has been an elder for thirty years already. We are not told what to do if the child of an elder sins significantly, but repents just as thoroughly, and is now walking with the Lord in the state penitentiary. We are not told if the passage applies to an elder whose five natural children are all faithful, but the crack cocaine baby they adopted when she was just a toddler has completely fallen away. Suppose the wayward child is the oldest, a stepson to the minister, and all *his* children are faithful. One of the reasons we need judicious and godly men to be our elders is that they must make decisions like this. And I grant that the right process for dealing with all such tangles is not easy, simplistic, or formulaic.

I also grant that there are textual and broader theological issues. What about Jacob's children? They were kind of a mess, especially Levi—destined for ministry. And then King David had a bunch of kids that we wouldn't exactly put on the cover of a homeschooling magazine. What about them? These guys can have kids that are a disaster zone, and they can write a bunch of the Bible, but if a man has a kid who is only one tenth that bad, he can't preach from that same Bible? Okay, I get it.

But if we want reformation in our time—and we should—we need to return to the Bible, whether or not we are flattered by what we discover there. Our task should be to seek out what faithful obedience in this area might mean, what it might look like, and then to obey. This obedience is not just to be found at the individual or familial level. This is an area where the entire church needs to be involved in learning together, and coming together. Until we come to a consensus on how to draw this particular line, we will continue to be frustrated by a pandemonium of voices from every direction.

Suppose we tentatively set a very straightforward standard. Suppose we said that if the child of an elder or minister is ever excommunicated, then the elder or minister in question will submit his resignation. And if there are extenuating circumstances—as there will sometimes be, no doubt—then the decision about any exceptions will be referred to presbytery, outside the context of the local church. We would be applying the wisdom the Westminster theologians showed on the subject of divorce—saying that in such tangles those most closely involved should not be judges in their own cases. Suppose we started with something like that?

I want to argue for this kind of approach in the sections that follow, and I do want to cover the subject as thoroughly as I can.

As has been said, obedience is the great opener of eyes. Drawing the line in the wrong place is preferable to refusing to draw it at all. Once we start doing something together when a child is excommunicated, we might be in a position to deal with, say, high scandal repented of. As we begin to obey, the Lord may continue to give us more obedience. But in order to wade in from the shallow end of the pool, we do have to get into the pool in the first place.

CHAPTER 1

Leaving the Ninety-Nine

Over the years I have written a good deal about the great neglected qualification for the ministry. Paul tells us plainly that a man whose house is not in order is not qualified to be a steward in the household of God. The stewardship abilities required in the one setting are comparable to those which are needed in the other. The texts seem plain enough.

But having stated the hard center of the position, let us go on to acknowledge that life is messy and the texts are not plain enough to apply themselves. Somebody has to make decisions about it, and there will be complications. For example, the requirements have to do with making someone a minister—sacking a minister two years before his retirement is not in view. We also have to decide where the enforcement line for others might be. A man might have one line for what would require his own resignation, another one for how much he would say if a friend asked his advice, and yet a third for what he would fight about at presbytery.

Another question concerns what scale of blameworthiness we are using—do we wait until excommunication? Or is the line crossed as soon as the wife of the head deacon sees the teenaged son of the minister sneaking into the back room of the video rental store? Okay, so life is messy, and we have to make decisions, and we have to do so non-legalistically, and do so without treating personal pastoral problems like we were stacking no more than five wooden blocks. Got it.

That said, I want to offer another consideration for men who are in such messy situations, and who truly desire to know what the Lord would have them do. I do not offer them a rule, and certainly I am not handing a rule over to the self-appointed chairman of their lynching party. I don't want to lend encouragement to any "tag, you're disqualified" factions within the church. Sometimes people confuse settling scores with holiness. I simply offer something to consider, and here it is.

Not all disqualifications are the same. Some men are disqualified from the ministerial office down to the bone. Given the nature of the case, they are probably disqualified in other areas as well, but when it comes to the Christian family, they don't have a clue.

Many years ago, back in our Jesus-people days, when I was a very young pastor, a gent rolled into town, and "felt led" to join in with us on the leadership team. Only problem was, he had been married six times—and the last two wives were in his Christian phase. Um, let us think about it, no.

Let's say a pastor has six kids, all of them hellions, from the three-year-old, whom the child care workers at the church have affectionately named Demon Child, to the eldest boy, who is sixteen and has already gotten three girls in the youth group pregnant. How all this could possibly be happening is a grand mystery to

Dad, and he feels greatly put upon if anybody is legalistic enough to bring it up. Whatever happened to grace? This is disqualification *simpliciter*.

But there is another sort of qualification issue that is in a different category entirely. It is not the revealing of an utterly unpastoral heart, but is rather closer to what I would regard as one of a pastor's final qualifying exams, an advanced test. A pastor has a number of grown children, walking in the Lord, and one black sheep. Does the Bible give directions to shepherds about the sheep who can take care of themselves for a bit, and the one who obviously can't? Yes, it does.

"What man of you, having an hundred sheep, if he lose one of them, doth not leave the ninety and nine in the wilderness, and go after that which is lost, until he find it? And when he hath found it, he layeth it on his shoulders, rejoicing" (Luke 15:4-5).

There are two elements here—the obvious one is finding the lost sheep. But the other element is that of leaving the ninety nine. In this scenario, with this consideration, the disqualification would not be in the fact of the sheep wandering—that does happen from time to time. The potential disqualification comes in not going after the wandering sheep. The "reveal" is not found in the fact that a pastor's kids can sin, sometimes grievously. I would want to argue that a pastor's kid can sin grievously without disqualifying his or her father from the ministry. But what happens after that? When a child sins in this way, it is not so much a disqualification from ministry as it is a drastic invitation to radical ministry.

So this is just a consideration. When should a good pastor leave the 99? "For the Son of man is come to seek and to save that which was lost" (Luke 19:10). The answer is some form of "when there are just 99."

CHAPTER 2

Generational War

Many conservative Christians know that the culture war we are fighting is a desperate battle for our children. Now fighting for your children and grandchildren is a noble enterprise. It is what we are called to do. When such fighting is necessary, as in a fallen world it constantly is, it is something we are called to do for the sake of others, and this includes our children.

"And I looked, and rose up, and said unto the nobles, and to the rulers, and to the rest of the people, Be not ye afraid of them: remember the Lord, which is great and terrible, and fight for your brethren, your sons, and your daughters, your wives, and your houses" (Neh. 4:14).

But as good as this is, we need to move past it. Once we realize that we are in a long war, a war in which the first blood shed was that of Abel, and the last blood shed will be that of the final martyr, an honored someone who will no doubt not be born for many centuries yet, we will finally recognize the importance of the time we are called to invest in our children.

Because it is a long war, it crosses generations. In a very short space of time, your children will join you in the line, and a short time after that, their children will join them. This means that we begin by fighting for our children, but we must end by fighting by means of them. We must do two things simultaneously—we must fight today's battles, and we must recruit and train tomorrow's warriors.

If I am alloted more than the proverbial three score and ten, I hope that as my children and grandchildren are hitting their stride, and I will see myself as still fighting through them.

I see this in my own father—still fruitful in his own ministry—whenever he hears of any skirmish or battle that his descendants have gotten into. He is an old war horse, restless in his stall, wanting to get into it himself. But he actually is "into" it. None of us would be where we are now without him, and I hope that I have the same privilege that he has been given—that of seeing a lot of downstream damage to the work of the adversary.

Decades from now, when my descendants are giving fits to whatever progressives are calling themselves in the 22nd century, I hope that my name is a hissing and a byword to God's enemies.

So a short-sighted man who throws himself into ministry, neglecting his family in order to do so, is not just demonstrating for us that he doesn't understand his wife and kids. He is demonstrating for us the fact that he doesn't understand the nature of true ministry.

The command for elders to have faithful children is not just thrown in there as a mindless rule, so that ecclesiastical fussbudgets might have something to agitate about during elder elections. If a man's children don't care what he believes about the Bible, then why should we? This is a line of argument that Paul endorses. If his children have walked away from what he says is important about the Bible, but we are still hanging on to his every word, the chances are good that we have adopted a false and unbiblical set of weights and measures, and are hanging on to the wrong words, or to good words for the wrong reasons.

Jesus said that we were to evaluate teachers by the kind of fruit they produced. And what better place to check than their garden at home? A man who is wrong about children will find it difficult to be right about anything else.

So what we need (as I've said in other places) are more children with the right kind of bright in their eyes, like Jonathan after he ate the honey. But in his case, it was in spite of his father's foolish prohibition. May God spare us from the indignity of having children who do well despite us. We want children who have that kind of bright in their eyes because they have fathers who gave them the honey in the first place.

CHAPTER 3

Exceptions and the Rule

In the first place, the apostle Paul teaches us that how a man behaves in his home is a predictor or indicator of how he will behave in the church. If you want a godly and competent leader in the church, then you need to look for a godly and competent leader in his home. The apostle couldn't make his point plainer.

"For if a man know not how to rule his own house, how shall he take care of the church of God?" (1 Tim. 3:5). The word rendered rule here is *proistemi*, which means preside, rule, maintain. And the word used with regard to pastoral work is *epimeleomai*, which means to take care of, or provide for.

This is a simple *if, then* statement. If a man does not know how to do x, then he will not be able to do y. We will examine what that connection is later, but it should suffice for the present to show that there is such a connection. We should refuse to call a pastor based on certain realities in his home, and we should do this as a matter of obedience to God. If a pastoral candidate were not very good at racketball, or was not a competent hunter, or had never been hang-gliding, we would not be within our rights to say that obedience required us to reject him. There would *not* be a connection between these activities and the possibility of him being a good pastor, and there *is* a connection between him being a good father and being . . . a good father. This is obvious.

But another obvious thing is that the world is a messy place, and that application of this qualification requires that we make judgment calls. Some of the judgment calls will be more difficult to make than others. This requirement is not like the requirement that our Constitution sets for the president being 35-years-old (Art. II). All you have to do to determine if the qualification is met is be able to count. Or to take an example from the Old Testament, the requirements for the priesthood were more objective and physical (Lev. 21:16-21), and therefore easier to check..

But what we must not do here is set these two obvious things at odds with each other. We must not assume that because there is a requirement that a man manage his household well, that there will never be difficulties in deciding what to do. Simplistic thinking is the badge of the legalist. But neither may we acknowledge that there will be hard cases, and conclude from this that the familial qualification is functionally meaningless. The requirement must be held as a real requirement—meaning that certain men are kept out of office because of it, and they are men who otherwise would be ordained to office.

So how do we balance these two things? There is a legal adage that says that hard or difficult cases make bad law. You should let the simple requirement drive the majority of your cases, and deal with your exceptional cases as they arise.

There is another adage that says that the exception proves the rule, but this adage is almost universally misunderstood. The phrase is frequently taken as the exception somehow *establishing* the rule, with the word *proves* taken in the sense of what you do to get to a conclusion in an argument. But the proverb was developed when the word *prove* had the meaning of *test*. The exception *tests* the rule.

Let me give you a made up example that will show how an exception can be made which tests, or honors, the rule, and then make up another example where it does nothing of the kind.

Say the congregation is considering a pastoral candidate, and it comes out in the interview that when he was 19, shortly before he became a Christian, he was shacked up with a girl for six months. She got pregnant and left him because she was a strident atheist and didn't like the spiritual direction he was taking. He has had no legal recourse, and his son from that union was brought up as an atheist, and is one screwed-up kid. After your candidate was converted, he finished college, went to seminary, and met his current wife while studying for the ministry. They married, and have five lovely children, all of whom love God, love Jesus, love their parents, and love church.

Now suppose you have another candidate, one who has five children, two of whom are sullen and disobedient. The other three might be okay, you think. But the two are bad attitudes with sneakers, laces untied. The pastoral candidate is the photo negative of the centurion in the gospels (Matt. 8:9). When the father saith come, the child goeth. When he saith go, the child cometh. When he says do this, the teen-ager doeth it not.

In the first example, the exception tests the rule—it makes you think hard about the rule, and it makes you see how the rule actually still applies. We are checking to see how this man manages the children he has, not how he was a father to a child he never had the opportunity to father. It is easy to see how the pastoral search committee could determine that his atheist son (whom he had met three times in his life) was not the kind of situation that the apostle Paul had in mind. With the children he has, the congregation can see how he rules in his household, and they can expect that he would take care of them on that basis.

But in the second situation, you can immediately see that the two exceptions were not instances that tested the rule—they were instances where the rule excluded the candidate. The bad things you saw in the household meant that if you called such a man, you should expect to see bad things in the church, bad things that were somehow related to his weakness in his home.

So the requirement in 1 Tim. 3:5 is clear, but requires wisdom to apply. And the application of wisdom should never be treated as though it were relativism.

CHAPTER 4

Background Assumptions

One of things we need to do in our discussion of family qualifications for ministry is examine some of our background assumptions. As with many other issues, our understanding of Paul's requirement here (1 Tim. 3:2-5; Tit. 1:5-6) is affected not only by what the text clearly says, but by the eyes we bring to the text. What we see is sometimes a function of what is there to be seen, and other times a function of how good our eyesight is. There are times when certain assumptions about what the text "could not *possibly* be saying" will shape what we allow it to say to us.

One of those background assumptions (for moderns) is individualism. Now of course God did create us as distinct individuals, and we go to Heaven or Hell by ones. Moral responsibility is fundamentally located in the individual. But there is more to moral responsibility than that. Our lives are intertwined, and this is particularly the case when we are talking about parents and their children—the philosopher René Girard calls us interdividuals.

When we consider the scriptural examples, there are many instances of wayward children, which we will look at in due course. But one of the things we must do is look at what is exactly happening with these scriptural examples—and we are not left in the position of having to guess. Sometimes we are just told what happened (as when Jacob's sons sinned over the rape of their sister). But other times, we are also told *why*—and not surprisingly, in certain cases, it was a matter of parental negligence.

Let's look at a couple of examples, and then move on to some general statements that are made in Scripture about this.

In the period of the judges, an unnamed man of God once came with a message to Eli, chastising him for preferring to honor his sons over the Lord (1 Sam. 2:29). And in the next chapter, the first prophetic message that Samuel had to deliver was one of judgment to Eli, because his sons had "made themselves vile" and he had not restrained them (1 Sam. 3:13). Now it is true that Eli did eventually deliver a verbal rebuke, but that was plainly an instance of too little, and too late (1 Sam. 2:22-23).

Another example is how David brought up his sons. Adonijah had a lot going for him, but one of his problems was that David had never crossed his will. "And his father had not displeased him at any time in saying, Why hast thou done so?" (1 Kings 1:6). Keep in mind that David's sons were also priests—not in the public cult tended by the Levites, but probably within David's palace (2 Sam. 8:18, ESV).

In these instances, Eli's sons and David's were clearly responsible for their own sin. They were responsible moral agents. But they had gotten into the position they were in because of what their father had not done in how he had brought them up. Their responsibility was individual, certainly, *but it was not solitary*. There was a shared responsibility in this on the part of Eli and David.

We have already acknowledged the reality of certain exceptional cases. But we also have to remember that there are proverbial cases, general truths. For example, a son who is lazy during harvest is a son who brings shame (Prov. 10:5). Shame to whom? Clearly, the answer is that he brings shame to his parents. This is not a lazy man who brings shame to himself; he is a lazy *son*.

An industrious servant is going to be privileged in the inheritance over a son who causes shame (Prov. 17:2). Again, this is referring to shame coming upon the parents. And a son who is a wastrel is a son who brings shame (Prov. 19:26).

Now as already noted, individuals can certainly bring shame down on their own heads. It is shameful to answer a matter before you have heard it out (Prov. 18:13). To throw yourself into controversy hastily is shameful (Prov. 25:8). And of course, pride and haughtiness is a set up for shame (Prov. 11:2). But when the shameful person is being considered as a child, that shame is shared. And it is shared for a reason.

"The rod and reproof give wisdom: *But a child left to himself* bringeth his mother to shame" (Prov. 29:15).

In the instances cited above, the shame comes to pass when the child is older. The shameful son is old enough to work the harvest, and doesn't. He is old enough to receive an inheritance, and the servant gets it before he does. He is old enough to run up his parents' credit card.

And in the examples from the households of Eli and David, the problems were adult problems, but the causes had been laid down many years before. A child left alone brings shame, and that leaving alone is something that can start happening as soon as the child is born and able to be left alone. Leave a two-year-old kid alone, and bad things start happening. What do you have to do to have a garden fill up with weeds? Well, nothing, as it turns out.

So, then, we want to avoid the charge of wooden legalism in this matter. A wooden legalist would be someone who cannot allow any sort of complication or exception. He thinks the law of God is made out of pressure-treated two by fours. But we must also acknowledge that God teaches us that it is generally true that a child who is brought up poorly is more likely to turn out poorly. To reason from the fact of some exceptions to a desire to have the proverbial wisdom *never* apply is to choose squishy relativism over wooden legalism. But the law of God is not made out of orange jello either.

The proverbs I have sited are *proverbs*. They are not "all triangles have three sides" kinds of statements. But proverbs are still generally true, or at least the good ones are. A stitch in time *usually* saves nine. A little sleep, a little slumber, a little folding of the hands to rest, and once in a blue moon you win the lottery—but don't count on it. You should count on something else.

Now because proverbs are generally true, we may be assured that a father like Eli, who has trouble confronting his sons, will have trouble confronting others in the church who need to be confronted. How the family is managed is, the apostle Paul teaches, a predictor of what you can expect within the congregation. To expect in one place what you saw in the other is a *reasonable* expectation.

CHAPTER 5

Two Ditches

I have said in other contexts that the Pauline requirements for ministry are character qualifications, and as such they are not analogous to the operation of counting rocks.

Though we are discussing the requirement of godly family management, let me illustrate the point with one of the other qualifications, also having to do with family. Paul says that an elder must be a one-woman man. This sounds great, but what do we mean. Ever? It is obvious that we must draw a line at some point, and the first thing to do is admit this fact to ourselves. If we do not admit it, we will still draw that line, but the fact that we have done so will be invisible to us, and it will be entirely arbitrary.

For example, say that a man has been presented as a candidate for elder, and he has been married to the same woman, happily, for the last thirty years. But, when he was a young man, before he was a Christian, he was married to someone else who left him and divorced him after six months. This fact will be an item for discussion in his elder candidacy (as it should be). The question will be whether or not this man qualifies as a one-woman-man. Fine.

But suppose there is another candidate who slept with twenty-one women before his conversion, but was enough of a jerk not to marry any of them. He too is happily married now, and his past is treated in the elder election as a matter of irrelevance. But Paul doesn't say "one-woman-man in marriage." He says one woman man.

Now if you think you are counting rocks instead of evaluating character you will soon be at a point where you are not even able to count the rocks. You will think that the gold sanctifies the altar, and not the other way around. You will disqualify a man for being with two women in his life, and allow a man who has been with twenty-two women.

When we are looking at a man's family, we are looking for what we want to see duplicated—for Paul tells us that it will be duplicated. So let me give a couple of examples that might test whether we think the altar sanctifies the gold or the gold the altar.

Let us say that a minister's brother and sister-in-law are killed in a car accident. They were not believers, and their 15-year-old daughter was brought up in a thoroughly pagan environment. She comes to live with her believing uncle and aunt, and they of course have a number of challenges. Sexual activity is something she just assumes, along with liberal drug use, though nothing too hard. They are doing what they can with a hard situation, and the minister's own kids are all doing great. Now is this man qualified to be a minister unless and until he adopts his niece? As soon as he adopts her, someone might say, jabbing at Titus 1, he has an unbelieving daughter. Sure, the response comes, but *why*? The reason he has an unbelieving daughter is that he is the kind of man you want shepherding the flock.

Suppose you have a similar scenario, only this time the minister and his wife take in a foster daughter who is a four-year-old. She was a crack cocaine baby, and her mom has been with seventeen different men during the course of her short life. She is taken in as an act of true mercy, and her foster parents are being Jesus to her. Would being Jesus disqualify them? Or would it disqualify them as soon as they decided to adopt her fully, instead of keeping her at the arm's length distance of foster child? To think that such a thing would disqualify a man is to aspire to get one of those Fools-and-Blind awards that we see Jesus dispensing in the gospels.

At the same time, Paul did not give us these requirements in the Pastorals so that we could spend all our time thinking up ingenious exceptions to them. There is such a thing as mismanagement of a family, it is fairly common, and we can see it in the result of insolent and disobedient children. We can even see it in the complicated dynamics of the situations I described above. Suppose a minister adopts more scrambled kids than he can handle, and he loses both them and his natural children, who drift away from the Lord in bitterness and jealousy. That's not good either. A minister is not qualified in the broader church because he made of hash of things but meant well.

As I am fond of saying, there is a ditch on both sides of the road. In the circles I travel in, I see examples of both. In one ditch, wayward ministerial children are an unfortunate norm. It is already this way in the broader evangelical and Reformed world, and it is becoming increasingly acceptable in the conservative, family-oriented Reformed world. But it really shouldn't be.

But in the other ditch, you have small churches that have such tight standards for the family of the elder that the church struggles along without any leadership at all. This kind of hyper-scrupulosity contrasts sharply with Paul's actual practice. If you look at the time line carefully in one portion of Paul's ministry, he appointed elders after about three weeks of ministry, right before he left town (Acts 14:23). Here is your Bible, these are the standards, seeya. I'll write.

CHAPTER 6
High Standards at the Front End

As we continue to consider the implications of Paul's requirements for the minister's family, a few other considerations need to be introduced. These considerations are not in the interest of governing through exceptions—just the reverse, actually.

We are coming (soon enough) to a statement of what this high standard means in application, and when we get there, the discomfort levels will be as high as the standard is. There are many ministers and elders who are not qualified to hold the office that they do, and they are not qualified because of the spiritual condition of their children. When we get to that point, I want it to be as plain as it could possibly be that the expectation of a godly family is not wooden legalism. This means granting the complications and exceptions first.

That said, the apostle is teaching us about the selection of elders. This is what the requirement is at the front end, which cannot be applied straight across once a man has been ordained and installed. There is a corollary to this, which is that the more tightly the biblical standards are held at the front end, the less frequently will you have a bad and awkward situation with an existing officer.

If you are going to be picky, the place to do it is when you are making your selection. Think of marriage and divorce as an example. A man might decide not to pursue a woman because of the color of her hair, or her height, which he has every right to do. But he cannot use such criteria in deciding whether to divorce her. The doorway in and the doorway out are not the same door.

In the same way, someone might vote against an elder candidate because he is too excitable, not dignified enough. This is part of the Pauline expectation for the church officer. A man must be sober, temperate (Tit. 1:8). In the judgment of the person who votes no, the man concerned lacks the judicious temperament that he will need to help govern the church. Let us also say, for the sake of the discussion, that this person voting no is correct in his assessment, but that the congregation votes the other way, and the man is ordained as an elder. This is not the end of the world; what we have is a simple disagreement.

Once in office, let us say that the fact he has the wrong kind of temperament becomes increasingly and gradually obvious. It was obvious to the man who voted no on the first day, but once the man is ordained, that man should wait patiently until it becomes obvious to others.

It is the same with a man's family. It is not the case that once a man is installed, he is like a termite in the woodwork. We should not see ordination as an irreversible affair. Churches are bound together by covenant, and the terms of the covenants we are to use are set down for us in Scripture. A man might be kept out of office because of the state of his family, or he might be removed from office because of the state of his family. But given the nature of the case, those thresholds should be in different places.

If two-thirds of the congregation vote against a man because they "had a feeling in their gut" about that man's surly teenage daughter, they have every right to do so. If they do, he will be kept out of office. But if that man is already in office, then the existing government of the church is required not to entertain a charge against an elder except on the word of two or three witnesses (1 Tim. 5:19).

Before he is in office, views about his family are a judgment call. After he is in office, they are a charge. Beforehand, nothing needs to be proven. A feeling in the gut is fine. Voting no is not the same as bringing a charge. Afterward, in order to remove a man because of his family, everything needs to be proven. That is, everything needs to be proven if the man is of a mind to make everybody prove what ought to be obvious.

This leads to one of the more important characteristics that a minister or church officer needs to have. Before a man accepts the office, he needs to determine that he will not cling to it desperately if his family starts to wobble. He needs to be the first one to suggest stepping down, and not the last one sitting in a deserted church building with the lights out. We will consider this more in detail later, but he needs to be the kind of shepherd who will leave the 99.

I knew, growing up, that if I or any of my siblings walked away from the Lord, my father would be out of the ministry later that afternoon. And I knew this without it feeling like emotional blackmail—the apostle Paul teaches that masters should "forebear threatening," and so I am not suggesting that a man should use his vocation and livelihood as a cudgel on his children ("If you kids don't continue to love Jesus, your mother and I will be on food stamps"). My wife and I had that same standard with regard to our children. And we still do, even though they are grown. As for me and my house, we will serve the Lord.

One of the things you should want in the culture of the church is for the elders to be harder on themselves in this regard than the congregation is. The opposite disposition, where the congregation is critical and the minister defensive, is an explosion waiting to happen. And when it happens, it will be ludicrous—a congregation wanting a minister to step down because one of his daughters wore lipstick once, or a minister not wanting to step down even though three of his four sons are in the penitentiary.

If you have the right kind of man, the subject will be broached first by him, and not by his ecclesiastical adversaries. At the same time, the congregation should not be so emotionally attached to their pastor that they prevent him from obeying the apostle even though it has become manifestly obvious that it is past time to step down.

Reformation in the church is not going to come in the church as a result of us preventing the next wave of unqualified ministers—think homosexual ordination. Reformation will be the result of us dealing with the previous waves of unqualified ministers. We need to be more concerned about our past compromises than our future ones.

CHAPTER 7

Congregational Support

The calling of a pastor can be a demanding, rigorous, and often thankless calling. For every televangelist with white shoes raking it in, there are a hundred men laboring in obscure corners of the Lord's vineyard.

For those who are aware of this reality—the fact that congregations are sometimes critical, fussy, envious, and spiteful—to adopt strict views of the minister's qualifications in how he governs his household seems to be just asking for it. The family already lives in a fishbowl, people are already wondering why his wife doesn't play the piano, and more than one comment has been made about how infrequently their teen-aged son has to mow the lawn. Why would anyone volunteer to make "the treatment" worse than it already is?

The answer is that the requirement is in the Bible, and so there must be a way of doing it right. But doing it right does not just mean having a conscientious pastor, or a conscientious session, but also a faithful and wise congregation. If they are wise, they will know (because they have been taught) the difference between responsibility and humiliation. When a minister's child starts to waver, the congregation wants to know who to help, not who to blame.

Let me illustrate the heart of the point without reference to a minister. All parents are parents of children who sin. This is a fact of life. When we live in community, those sins will be visible and apparent to others. Wise and godly parents deal with it, taking it in stride. Parents who are still dealing with things on the surface are embarrassed by it.

In a social setting, a child being hauled off to be corrected should be as unremarkable as a child being taken to have his diapers changed. These things happen, and good parents know that they are responsible to deal with it. But if, instead of dealing with it, they are simply ashamed of it, they are inviting others to blame them instead of helping them.

My wife and I have the great privilege of seeing our sixteen grandchildren interact with one another on a regular basis. There is a good bit of terryhooting and good times, but cousin sin has been known to occur. If our response is "Oh no! Sin!" then we simply do not know what kind of world we are living in. One of the greatest blessings of our lives is that of watching our children as parents give a heads-up to one another about some developing state of moral disorder at the two-foot grandkid level, with nobody getting defensive. Just doing the business.

The point is this. If a congregation expects to have a minister or elders with sinless children then their expectations are radically unbiblical. The issue is not whether or not sin occurs, but rather what happens when it does. The issue is not sin, the issue is sin unaddressed with efficacious love. When the sin is flamboyant enough, this is usually an indication that a catalog of previous sins were going on unaddressed. But the issue is not the mess, but rather the unwillingness or inability to clean it up.

The men who govern the flock are shepherds, and this is what shepherds are supposed to do. This is their calling.

"And he spake this parable unto them, saying, What man of you, having an hundred sheep, if he lose one of them, doth not leave the ninety and nine in the wilderness, and go after that which is lost, until he find it? And when he hath found it, he layeth it on his shoulders, rejoicing. And when he cometh home, he calleth together his friends and neighbours, saying unto them, Rejoice with me; for I have found my sheep which was lost" (Luke 15:3-6).

One of the things that our session of elders has done over the years is provide practical help to men who have to face challenges in their families. To make up an example, suppose that an elder discovers that his oldest boy has a significant porn problem, and he has three boys younger than that coming up. He doesn't know how all this is going to go, and knows that he has some work to do. Such an elder could ask for and receive a six month leave of absence from his responsibilities as an elder. *This is not six months in the penalty box.* This is so that instead of being a shepherd who continues to tend the ninety nine, he could be released to be a shepherd who is pursuing the one.

A true willingness to pursue the one is often all it would take to win back that one. I am making no universal claims, but I am making some claims about a significant number of ministers' kids. If a child has grown up resentful of his father's ecclesiastical busyness, and for him the name of Jesus means that he has to look at the back of Dad's head going off to another damn meeting—because *every* problem in the church outranks *any* problem of his, no matter how serious—then it should not be a great shock to discover that such a child eventually just wanders off. The question in that child's heart is, "At what point would Dad drop everything and come after me?" The answer appears to be *never*.

There are practical and logistical issues connected with this, as you might well imagine. And that is why it is important for a whole community to share the same values, to live in the same wisdom and love, and to provide godly opportunities for the shepherds to pursue sheep, especially if those sheep are in their own family. If a man is pursuing a wayward son, for example, that would not be a good time for the ninety-nine to start a church fight over supralaparianism, the right use of the deacons' fund, or the color of the carpet in the nursery.

CHAPTER 8

The Standard
in Action

U p to this point someone might be excused for thinking my purpose in tackling this issue of elder qualifications in a man's family has been to explain to us all what the standards do not mean, and all the circumstances where they *don't* apply. This has been a regrettable necessity because our modern approach to this subject is likely to fall into one of two extremes. Either we have our shoes laced up so tight that we find ourselves incapable of finding anyone who is qualified to be in church leadership at all, and so we struggle along with that form of unbiblical government. Or we lapse into the common view that the ministry is just another profession, and how a man's children are doing has nothing whatever to do with his craft competence. But an ability to take tests at a graduate school level is not the same thing as leading and shepherding people.

This is why I began where I did. I trust that I've shown I don't make *clunkity clunkity* noises as I do the exegesis of Titus 1 and 1 Tim. 3. Now it is time to begin addressing what the standards do in fact mean, and to begin dealing with some of the excuses we have developed for not obeying them. And this is what it comes down to at the end of the day—obedience.

Since we have been addressing those situations where wisdom really must be used in how we apply the passages, let's start by considering those areas where expedience suggests we do nothing, and suggests we take a pass in the name of wisdom. Here are some of the evasions that come readily to mind

1. The minister's children are grown and out of the home. The qualifications do not apply.

In fact, the standards as they are given in Titus assume that the children in question are older. The elder's children must not be accused of debauchery or rebellion. Now you occasionally meet a two-year-old that brings such words to mind, but generally this would refer to someone who is capable of being out of the home.

And who cannot see that the harvest tells us something about the time of plowing and planting? Scripture teaches us to judge by the later fruit, which speaks about the earlier root.

2. The minister's children are small, and still at home. The qualifications do not apply.

In addition to being at the other end from the previous objection, this still fails. Though fruit is harder to identify when the children are little, and granting that some fussers think any happy home with a bunch of kids is by definition disorderly, it is still possible to have a manifestly mismanaged home when the kids are little. So remembering what we addressed earlier, we have to distinguish between sin that is addressed promptly and in love, and sin that is just left there, festering.

Say that a five-year-old boy is insolent to his mother, in the presence of his father, the pastor, and he does this during the fellowship hour after church, in front of about twenty people. If dad hauls him off to the Star Chamber immediately, all twenty observers should go home reassured. Their pastor's kids sin, and their pastor deals with it. But if that sin happens in front of everybody, and mom goes off humiliated, and dad looks at his son with disgust, and then continues his conversation, there ought to be about twenty thought bubbles over about twenty heads, with the word "Yikes!" inscribed in them.

In a situation like this, incidentally, I don't believe that a minister ought to be removed. But I do believe that a wise session will require him to read books, take classes, or get some mentoring, because they see the disqualification coming and they want to head it off. This is the sort of situation that I think would disqualify a man from becoming an elder, but not be grounds for removing him. But it is only grounds for not removing him if something proactive is being done, something that will be effective.

3. I feel sorry for him, and for his wife, who is wonderful, and so harried by everything. The last thing they need right now is for him to lose his job.

In the first place, the ministry is not a job. It is a calling, and those who labor in that calling answer to the Lord who called them. Tending your family is an essential part of that vocation. It is not our "position," which we can alter or adjust as we see fit.

Second, as I tell people in counseling from time to time, there is no situation so bad but that you can't make it worse. Once it becomes obvious, postponing the hard talk or the hard decision usually makes things worse for everybody. You can do the hard thing now, or a much harder thing later.

Third, we need to start leaning against the common Christian tendency to assume that whenever a Christian is hired by Christians, a sort of automatic tenure sets in. Our vocation is our calling, and when we are called, it is to the Lord who called us. That calling summons us to efforts that reflect "my utmost for his highest," and not "Christians aren't perfect, just forgiven."

4. I don't have the votes on the session to remove him. Nobody else agrees with me.

This may well be the case. One faithful man might not have the votes to have an unqualified man removed. But one faithful man has the voice to ensure that if that minister is kept on, he will have been kept on through a conscious decision, and not because the fog of inertia kept anybody from saying anything.

Incidentally, I am not saying that a refusal to deal with a disqualified minister is grounds for leaving a church, although it may be. That depends on the circumstances. But I will say that one of the reasons why our informal means of dealing with church failures through church splits so common, is because we fail to be vocal about clear issues early on. There are many times when you can object, and still remain after the decision goes against you. But if you have kept silent for ten years over twenty issues, when the twenty-first issue bursts through the dam, you often discover that all the water behind that dam—and there is a lot of it—is toxic.

5. The minister is just a year from retirement. It would be heartless to require him to resign now.

The answer here is to not be heartless. Assuming the disqualification to be serious and obvious, there are still numerous ways to not be heartless and still honor the scriptural requirements. First, the fact that he is disqualified from pastoral ministry does not mean he is disqualified from everything. Have him teach history in your Christian school. In extreme circumstances, the church can take responsibility for finding a way, up to and including a generous severance package.

So what do we do? One of the things that I want to urge is for our churches to institute a standard that acknowledges the authority of Scripture in this, and which is formulated in the absence of a particular crisis.

For example, we could include a section in the church constitution that says something like "if a natural child of an elder or minister, having grown up in his father's house, is lawfully excommunicated by the church, the resignation of his father will be required at that same time." This would require positive action to prevent a resignation instead of positive action to initiate one. And while it does not cover all the instances where a resignation would be in order, it is a start, a step in the right direction.

CHAPTER 9

Drawing the Line

I have mentioned that we should begin any attempt to institute familial qualifications for the eldership with children who have been excommunicated. We could begin here for pragmatic reasons (we have to start somewhere), but I want to argue that there are exegetical grounds for having this be the place where we draw the basic line.

Here are the key words from Titus again. The elder must have "faithful children not accused of riot or unruly" (Titus 1:6). There are just eight words here in the English, but a lot rides on them.

Let's begin with "not accused." The minister's children must not be open to the charge of certain things. We will get to what those things are shortly, but the word underneath "accused" here is *kategoria*. It is a legal term, and has to do with the bringing of formal charges. It is not a word you would use to describe a couple of gossips whispering about the minister's son's girlfriend. This is the same word that is used when Paul tells Timothy not to admit a charge (*kategoria*) against an elder without two or three witnesses (1 Tim. 5:19). This is a place where the accusations are serious, and they are on the record.

The King James says that the charge that should not be able to be brought is the charge of riotous and unruly living. The words are *asotia* and *anypotaktos*, and we can get a sense of their meaning by looking at a range of translations. We find "dissipation or insubordination" (NKJV), "debauchery or insubordination" (ESV), or "dissipation or rebellion" (NASB). In other words, we are not talking about a child who has sinned by snitching his sister's quarter and is repentant. Rather, this is someone who is given over to high-handed sin, and who rebelliously refuses to repent.

Now let's look at a striking parallel to this in Deuteronomy 21.

> "If a man have a stubborn and rebellious son, which will not obey the voice of his father, or the voice of his mother, and that, when they have chastened him, will not hearken unto them: Then shall his father and his mother lay hold on him, and bring him out unto the elders of his city, and unto the gate of his place; And they shall say unto the elders of his city, This our son is stubborn and rebellious, he will not obey our voice; he is a glutton, and a drunkard. And all the men of his city shall stone him with stones, that he die: so shalt thou put evil away from among you; and all Israel shall hear, and fear." (Deut. 21:18-21)

Notice the parallels. You have a child of the covenant in both cases. You have remarkable similarity in the description of the sin involved. You have a judicial proceeding. You have a proceeding before the elders. And you have a terminal judgment. The one place that is not in parallel is the fact that this is something that happens with a family in Israel, and in Titus it is being applied to the family of a church officer. But before addressing that issue, let's consider all of these in order.

The fact that it is a covenant child in both instances can simply be noted. The sin involved is the same kind of thing. Take the Titus description of "debauchery and rebellion." The debauchery answers to "glutton and drunkard" and the rebellion answers to "stubborn and rebellious." The parents here bring their (clearly older) child before the elders, and they issue a judgment. In Titus, it is not stated who would bring the charge, but it would be a formal charge (*kategoria*). The elders of the town would address the situation in Deuteronomy, and the elders of the church would address the situation described in Titus. In Deuteronomy, the end of that sad affair would be execution. In 1 Cor. 5, the apostle Paul makes an interesting application of the Old Testament use of the death penalty. In Christian churches, excommunication is the fulfillment, the antitype, of the type of old covenant executions (1 Cor. 5:1-13). So instead of a carousing son of a minister being executed by the church at Crete, they would excommunicate him.

Titus is being required to appoint the kind of elders where this kind of scenario is extremely unlikely. Don't appoint elders who have children who *could* be charged in this way, with the subsequent proceedings bringing reproach upon the church. In order for the church to be above reproach, the new elders must be above reproach. And in order for the church to be above reproach, the existing elders would also need to be above reproach in this way also, because it would be a pretty bad spectacle for a sitting board of elders to exclude a new guy for having a dissolute son when half of *them* had dissolute sons.

In order to tidy this up a bit, a few other observations might be helpful. The Titus passage also requires that the elder have faithful or believing children. This understanding of "not excommunicated" helps us apply this standard without trying to peek into hearts. Virtually everywhere this adjective (*pistos*) appears as a descriptor of *persons*, it can be translated as "believing." But we don't need to rush off to set up a church tribunal that will determine if the elders' children believe in Jesus down to the very bottom of their hearts. We can simply accept a credible profession of faith, knowing that the works of the flesh are *manifest* (Gal. 5:19 ff.), and that if their profession is false, that will come out.

Now I have seen instances where this understanding is objected to strongly, and it is maintained that *pistos* can simply mean "reliable." On this view, it doesn't have to mean that the child has a credible profession of faith at all. But if Paul was not requiring a credible profession, but simply a kid who made his bed when told, who took out the trash when asked, and who did not sell cocaine in the high school parking lot after school, then I have a simple question. How many advocates of this reading have called for ministers to step down because their children were not reliable, in whatever sense they take that to mean? Why is it that virtually no ministers are ever asked to step down, even when the terms of Titus 1:6—on *their* reading—are fulfilled? I would suggest that something is deeply wrong, and reformation and revival would cause the fathers' hearts to turn to their children, and the children's hearts to the fathers.

But what about the one disparity, acknowledged earlier, between Deuteronomy and Titus? This actually makes the case for requiring this standard for church officers even stronger.

The Deuteronomy case concerned a family in Israel. What were all Israelite families required to do?

> "Now these are the commandments, the statutes, and the judgments, which the Lord your God commanded to teach you, that ye might do them in the land whither ye go to possess it: That thou mightest fear the Lord thy God, to keep all his statutes and his commandments, which I command thee, *thou, and thy son, and thy son's son,* all the days of thy life; and that thy days may be prolonged" (Deut. 6:1-2).

You, your son, and your grandson. Fearing the Lord, and keeping His statutes and commandments, was to be a family affair. This was the required norm. All of God's people were called to it.

Christian families in the new Israel are given the same standard. Children are to be submissive to their parents in all things—as a way of pleasing God (Col. 3:20). Christian fathers are required to bring their children up in the nurture and admonition of the Lord (Eph. 6:4). Christian children are to obey their parents in the Lord (Eph. 6:1).

This is for all of us. But since we are supposed to learn the harvest of all Christian living from those who are given spiritual responsibility for us (Heb. 13:7, 17), it makes sense that Paul would begin by requiring this of church officers. He requires it of church officers, not because it some super-spiritual weird thing, but rather because we should all be striving (in the grace of God) to have this be the norm. Leaders in the church are not called to super-spiritual living so that rank-and-file Christians don't have to worry about it. Rather, they are to set the pattern, so that other Christians might imitate them, as they imitate Christ. When it comes to life in our families, Christian leaders are the pace car.

CHAPTER 10

Even More (New) Issues

I f we adopt the policy I am suggesting in the larger church—that of asking elders and ministers to step down if their children are excommunicate (or the moral equivalent)—this solves some problems, but not all of them. It actually creates a few interesting problems.

One interesting problem it could create is that of establishing an institutional disincentive when it comes to excommunicating the children of elders and ministers. Say that the child in question richly deserves it, but everybody knows that if this happened his father would lose his position—so welcome to the world of perverse incentives. We don't want to get into a place where we disobey one text for the sake of obeying another one.

There is another issue. Drawing the line at excommunication does address the problem of overt disqualification in a minister's family, but it doesn't address the trickier problem of moral authority. Say that a pastor has three daughters, and say that every two years, three times in succession, they each got pregnant out of wedlock, from the oldest to the youngest. Say further that each of them repents honestly and fully, and is attending church regularly. One of them married the father, and the other two are single moms. Everyone is in fellowship. What about that?

This scenario, held up to the standard I am suggesting, means that their father the pastor doesn't have to step down. And that logic is quite sound. If we make excommunication the line, then if that line is not crossed, it is not crossed. I think this is quite true when it comes to the basic *moral* aspects of ministerial qualifications.

But there are other issues. Think of them as strategic qualifications. Think of it in terms of moral authority. A man can be qualified to be on the field—but that is not the same thing as being qualified to be the quarterback. Scripture says that Jesus taught with authority, and not like the scribes. Throughout church history, there have been many scribes who have held the ministerial office, and they have been nice guys. But because they were missing the kind of authority that knows how to lead men into battle, they gradually become ministerial caretakers.

Now scandal affects a man's moral authority. It saps his ability to make strong and decisive decisions. A situation arises where he must say or do something, but is reluctant because he knows what the comeback will be. When David heard that his son Amnon raped his daughter Tamar, he was furious. But he didn't act on that (righteous) anger because he had really snarled up his ability to do so through *his* sin with Bathsheba. He was forgiven, but his vigor, his perceptiveness, his authority, was greatly damaged.

Take this illustration one step out because David's sin with Bathsheba was his own sin. Say that Amnon's sin was the first high profile sin, and say that David dealt with it (barely) adequately, but not decisively. Now say that eight months later the son of a political rival in all the palace politics does the same thing. What has happened? David's ability to do what needs to be done has been adversely affected.

This means that how a man manages his household will spill over into some of the other qualifications. In Timothy, Paul says that he must be "blameless" and must have a "good report" with outsiders (1 Tim. 3:2,7). In Titus, the same kind of thing is urged, with the requirement of blamelessness bookending the requirement concerning his children (Tit. 1:6-7).

Now blameless does not mean *absolute* blamelessness in the sight of God. If God were to mark iniquities, who could stand (Ps. 130:3)? This is talking about reputational blamelessness.

And this is one of those unwieldy and uneven facts of life—scandals bounce the way punted footballs do. Fornication with pregnancy following is *not* a worse sin than fornication without pregnancy. But fornication with pregnancy following is usually far more *public*—which means that it can have more of a debilitating capacity when it comes to a man's ability to lead a congregation.

This is something that connects to the next point, something alluded to a bit earlier. What is the mission of the church? Every church should be actively involved in the evangelization of the town where they are located. The Christian faith is a religion of world conquest. It is not the case that Jesus told us to go out into all the world in order to establish and maintain an acceptable market share.

But it is easy—especially when real spiritual authority has started to slip away—to allow the real mission of the church to slip away with it. If the ministers of the churches are not up to the challenge of our assigned mission, then an obvious temptation will be to allow the mission of the church to drift over to something we *are* qualified to do.

This is why a minister who has stumbled (in his own life or in his management of his family) can be qualified to continue to serve in some aspect of God's kingdom work.

A minister in this position should first ask himself if he should be in the ministry at all. If the church adopts the position of not requiring such action unless there has been an excommunication, the minister himself should still have the authority to decide to take himself out of that position. If the decision is made to remain in ministry, I would suggest a thorough inventory or review of ministerial assignments and responsibilities. If this is done right, it could result in a man finding himself where he can labor far more effectively, and with greater authority.

As John Piper might put it, don't waste your shake up.

CHAPTER 11

Grace and the Home

In order for a minister's family to fit with the qualifications that Paul addresses in Timothy and Titus, there has to be a large measure of intentionality in it. Such families do not happen in fits of absentmindedness. The minister and his wife are obviously where it starts, but as the kids get older, they become part of the process. By the end, everyone in the family knows how much they like each other, but everyone also knows that this is connected to the Pauline requirements.

But there is a delicate balancing act required here. On the one hand, you don't want the kids to be oblivious to their position. A minister's family is an essential aspect of his ministry. To take an obvious example, a minister must be hospitable, and this is difficult if he has three sullen teenagers, glowering at the dinner table. Being a member of the minister's family is not a church office, but it is a key part of the church's ministry.

On the other hand, you don't want the whole matter of elder qualifications to turn into tangled forms of emotional blackmail and hostage-taking. "If you don't straighten up, young man, your dad will have to resign.

Why can't you think about anybody but yourself?"

The short answer to that question is that he has learned to think about himself by watching his parents closely. When he misbehaves, their first reaction is what it will mean to them. They are not thinking first about God and His Word, or second about what this sin might be doing to their brother and son. No, rather, the first impulse was to ask "How do you think this makes us feel?" But people aren't shamed into selflessness. If shame could make us good, we'd all be good by now.

Gospel ministry is ministry of gospel. Gospel has moral consequences, of course, and one of those consequences is an upright life. One of the consequences of apple trees is apples. Morality does not generate happiness. Happiness generates morality.

I grew up in a home where my parents held that Paul's requirements applied to them, straight across. I was the oldest of four, and if any of us walked away from the faith I knew that my father would step down from the ministry later that afternoon. But I never once felt threatened by this. I never felt like my parents were holding something over me. My kids had the same expectation growing up, and I once heard my son describe it not so much us holding something over him, as it was him being given something that he could hold over us— and which he was expected and trusted not to do.

So rightly cultivated, this standard grants responsibility to growing children. Applied the wrong way, it treats children as projects or exhibits, with virtually no freedom or responsibility at all.

Grace liberates, and all of God's standards are grace to us. We can receive them (disobediently) as something other than grace, and when we do, things start to go wrong. Law can condemn. Law can stir up additional rebellion. Law can be the stick that whacks the hornet nest of self.

But the law of the Lord is perfect, converting the soul. The law of God is the Word of the God who brought us out of the land of Egypt, out of the house of bondage. The law of God is the summary of love. Love does no harm to its neighbor and thus love fulfills the law.

This is why—since the standards Paul describes do need to be present in a minister's home—that home must be a haven of grace. There is no other way for these standards to take root. By the grace of God, a father must give his children the ability to stand upright. Law by itself cannot do this. Standards cannot do this. Uptight rigor can't do it. Putting on appearances for all the fault-finders in the congregation can't do it.

Grace is the blessing of God, and this is the only way.

APPENDIX

Ordaining Young Ministers

Some might assume from the foregoing that it is therefore not prudent for young ministers (and therefore ministers with young children) to be ordained. After all, we don't know how their kids will turn out, right? I don't believe that inference is true, and so this appendix is attached.

False understandings of the etymologies of words sometimes cause minor confusion or bad jokes. Only rarely does it cause significant problems, but one exception to this is the difficulty caused by some Christians who believe that only elderly men are qualified to be elders of churches. Not only does this mean that many capable men are excluded from leadership in the church for most of their lives, it also means that when some of them finally come into the pastoral ministry, they do this as older men, but still novices to the pastoral office. The purpose of this short essay is to show that this assumption is misguided, and that it mitigates against the very thing it wants to encourage, which is maturity in office.

Of course, the word *prebyteros*—usually translated elder—does carry the meaning "old man." But this is not the only meaning it carries. It can also refer to those who hold a particular office—and where the office derived its name provides us with a good example of the etymological fallacy. Where a word came from and what a word means are two different things entirely. In earlier (tribal and patriarchal) times it would have been older men who overwhelmingly would have held that office, and so it was natural that such a name would be given. But once the office and name are established, a young man can certainly step into it.

We have an exact parallel to this in our use of the word *senator*. The word is related to the Latin *senex* which means old man. The root *sen-* indicates age, and we get the words *senator*, *senile*, and *senior* from it. And yet obviously, a young man can be elected to office and become a senator. According to the U.S. Constitution, a senator has to be at least just out of his twenties. "No person shall be a Senator who shall not have attained to the age of thirty years" [Art.I/Sec. 3]. Thirty is young, but thirty can be a *senator*.

Another variation is seen in how *Thayer's Greek/English Lexicon* divides references to age signified by this word into at least three categories—the first is where two people are spoken of and one is the elder of the two (Luke 15:25). The elder brother (*prebyteros*) of the prodigal was still a young man. The second age reference is the obvious one under discussion—it refers to one advanced in life, a senior. And yet another usage is what we would call "forefathers."

So we see that the word refers to the one who holds a particular "rank or office," such as a member of the great council or Sandhedrin. The Sanhedrin was the body of elders for the nation of Israel. But there were local sanhedrins or courts as well.

> In a few cases, other words are substituted for *synedrion*, e.g. *presbyterion*, 'body of elders' (Luke 22:66; Acts 22:5), and *gerousia*, 'senate' (Acts 5:21). The councils (*synedria*) of Mt. 5:22, 10:17; Mk. 13:9, and the *boulai* of Jos., Ant. IV.8.14, etc. were local courts of at least seven elders, and in large towns up to twenty-three elders.[1]

This form of local and broader government developed by the Jews was picked up and extended by the early Christian church. Christian churches are sometimes called synagogues (Jas.2:2), and they certainly followed the same pattern of government (Acts 14:23). The church council in Acts 15 was a Christian Sanhedrin (Acts 15: 2, 4, 6, 22-23).

All this is relevant because we may note the age requirements the Jews had for such office, and we may see how the Christian church carried those requirements over. But to do so, we have to piece some things together. The Jews required that a man be thirty years old before he could be a member of the Great Sanhedrin. But thirty is comparatively young. Paul shows his membership in that body when he tells us how he voted in the persecution of the church. "I verily thought with myself, that I ought to do many things contrary to the name of Jesus of Nazareth. Which thing I also did in Jerusalem: and many of the saints did I shut up in prison, having received authority from the chief priests; and when they were put to death, I gave my voice against them" (Acts 26:9-10). The literal rendering of "gave my voice" is "cast

---

1. J.D. Douglas, ed., *New Bible Dictionary* (Grand Rapids, MI: Eerdmans, 1962), p. 1142.

a pebble," i.e. he is referring to his vote. Commenting on Acts 26:10, I. Howard Marshall says that the fact that Paul voted against the Christians indicated his membership in the great Sanhedrin. "Since, however, Paul is talking about his activity in Jerusalem, membership of the supreme Sanhedrin is no doubt indicated."[2]

The interesting thing here is that we know that Paul was a young man around this time. "And cast him out of the city, and stoned him: and the witnesses laid down their clothes *at a young man's feet*, whose name was Saul" (Acts 7:58). How young? Paul was born a Roman citizen, as he put it (Acts 22:27). There were two acts by Rome which established registration of citizenry at birth. The first was *lex Aelia Sentia* in 4 A.D. and the second was *lex Papia Poppaea* in 9 A.D.[3] If Stephen was martyred around A.D. 30, then this meant that Paul was likely in his mid-twenties. If he had been born before 4 A.D., then his citizenship would not have been registered at birth, so a birth date between 4 and 9 A.D. is most likely.

Paul had made a mark on his people from the very beginning. "My manner of life *from my youth*, which was at the first among mine own nation at Jerusalem, know all the Jews; Which knew me from the beginning, if they would testify, that after the most straitest sect of our religion I lived a Pharisee" (Acts 26:4-5). And so, although the Sandredrin limited membership to those who were at least thirty, there may have been an exception in

---

2. I. Howard Marshall, *Acts: Tyndale New Testament Commentaries* (Downers Grove, IL: InterVarsity Press, 1980), 393.

3. F.F. Bruce, *Paul: Apostle of the Heart Set Free* (Grand Rapids, MI: Eerdmans, 1977), 40.

Paul's case. As he put it once: "For ye have heard of my conversation in time past in the Jews' religion, how that beyond measure I persecuted the church of God, and wasted it: And profited in the Jews' religion above many my equals in mine own nation, being more exceedingly zealous of the traditions of my fathers" (Gal. 1:13-14).

Not only did Paul serve the God of Israel before his conversion to Christ at a young age, but we must also note that it was in the middle of this youthful persecution of the Church that God made him an apostle. And Paul did not consider himself an anomaly in this, but was more than willing to follow the same pattern in how he trained others for ministry. The principal example of this is the case of Timothy.

The apostle Paul died around A.D. 67 at the hands of Nero. Just before his death, he wrote his second letter to Timothy. In that letter he told Timothy to guard against *the sins of youth*. "Flee also youthful lusts: but follow righteousness, faith, charity, peace, with them that call on the Lord out of a pure heart" (2 Tim. 2:22). In 1 Timothy, the point is even more explicit.

> These things command and teach. *Let no man despise thy youth;* but be thou an example of the believers, in word, in conversation, in charity, in spirit, in faith, in purity. Till I come, give attendance to reading, to exhortation, to doctrine. (1 Tim. 4:11-13)

Not only are we told that Timothy is a young man here, but we are further told that it is the duty of a young minister to keep people from despising that youth, which is a natural mistake for the people to make when a *young* man is an *elder*. But the meaning of the chronology here is that we must make this point even stronger. Paul is calling Timothy a young man, one whose youth might be despised, in the mid-sixties. But Timothy had joined Paul *in ministry* about *twenty* years before. The first missionary journey occurred in the mid-forties, and Paul had probably met Timothy in the mission to Lystra and Derbe. When he came back through on the second journey, he picked Timothy up as a lieutenant in ministry (Acts 16:1-3). This means that Timothy probably joined Paul in ministry while in his mid-teens.

Timothy is still a young man (in his thirties) twenty years later, but he was a significant authority in the church. One of his duties was to oversee the appointment of elders (1 Tim. 3:1-7), as well as handling charges that might be brought against such elders (1 Tim. 5:19). Of course, Timothy was charged to remember his youth in how he addressed and exhorted those who were his elders (1 Tim. 5:1), but he was *still* called upon to exhort them pastorally. In short, Timothy was given a significant ministerial charge while still a young man, and so we are not permitted to think that youth, by itself, presents an obstacle to ministry.

And so what should our application be? Those who are called to the ministry of the Word are often called to that vocation from their youth. Samuel first heard the word of the Lord as a boy, and in the Christian era, cases like Charles Spurgeon come to mind, who began preaching while still a teenager. My own forehead reddens to think that my first sermon was delivered in a Lutheran church when I was seventeen-years-old. Somebody should have been paying closer attention than they were, but the fact remains that the call of preaching has been a weight on me since I was a small boy. Now the fact that someone is called from his youth does not mean that he should hold office from his youth. But it does mean that older saints around such a person may bring him into ministry early, and nurture him in his calling.

And so there are three points of application that I would suggest. The first is that collective maturity on a session of elders *is* desirable. While a conservative approach is to be applauded, it is important that it not be wooden. Timothy is told not to be hasty in the laying on of hands (1 Tim. 5:22), and a neophyte in the faith can cause havoc (1 Tim. 3:6). But if a session has a good number of gray heads, and a wise, collective gravity, then to bring the strength and energy of qualified young men into the context of that kind of ministry is not a *lesser* good, but rather a *higher* good. An eldership without such young men is handicapped in some significant respects.

Second, the age of the children of elders should not be something we take into consideration by itself. This is because to do so is to go beyond the requirements of Scripture. We should see the unwieldiness of such extensions almost immediately. What about an older man with younger children? What about an older man with older daughters, and then a young son? What about a childless older man who becomes an elder, and then his wife conceives? We need to keep it simple. The Bible requires that if a man has a household, then it must be managed well, and the congregation should know that it is managed well. If a man cannot do this, then how can he manage the household of God (1 Tim. 3:5)? But this knowledge is not to be established after eighty years.

And third, we may do all this with confidence if we have the commitment to maintain a biblical standard of qualification for all elders—to become elders in the first place according to relevant scriptural criteria, and then to maintain their position as elders after the fact, also in accordance with the appropriate scriptural criteria. If those in ministry have the commitment to maintain their qualifications in all diligence, this means that they have the commitment to step down from ministry should disarray in their household make it evident that they must do so. When this happens, it is a cause of grief, but it is also healthy for the church, and for the younger elders. A young man with young children should never view his ordination as the one hurdle he must get past, and then he is settled in the ministry for life.

In all these things, we should never forget that in the days of the new covenant, God promised to do a marvelous thing.

> And it shall come to pass in the last days, saith God, I will pour out of my Spirit upon all flesh: and your sons and your daughters shall prophesy, and *your young men shall see visions*, and your old men shall dream dreams: And on my servants and on my handmaidens I will pour out in those days of my Spirit; and they shall prophesy. (Acts 2:17-18)

So when we consider the godly maturity of a board of elders, age is obviously a factor. But it is not the only factor. Age by itself is not a guarantee of maturity, and youth does not guarantee immaturity. A young man can be wise beyond his years, and older men can be foolish. Age is a natural receptacle for wisdom and maturity, and we should desire such collective wisdom and maturity for our session of elders. But an essential part of this is learning how to bring young men into ministry in such a way that fifty years from now, we will not only have elders who are eighty-years-old, but also have elders who have been ministering to souls for fifty of those years. A sixty-year-old man who is made an elder may be wise in his household and business, but in the ministry he is still a novice.

If we want great wine decades from now, it is important to begin laying down the bottles now.

www.ingramcontent.com/pod-product-compliance
Lightning Source LLC
Chambersburg PA
CBHW060535030426
42337CB00021B/4276